A PRAIRIE BOY'S SUMMER

Also by William Kurelek

A PRAIRIE BOY'S WINTER
LUMBERJACK

A PRAIRIE BOY'S SUMMER

Paintings and Story by William Kurelek

1975

HOUGHTON MIFFLIN COMPANY BOSTON

Library of Congress Cataloging in Publication Data

Kurelek, William, 1927–
    A prairie boy's summer.
    SUMMARY: Text and twenty full color paintings
describe a young boy's summers on the Canadian
prairies during the 1930's.
    1. Canada — Social life and customs — Juvenile
literatures. 2. Children in Canada — Juvenile
literature. [1. Farm life — Canada. 2. Summer.
3. Canada — Social life and customs] I. Title.
F1021.K87 1975   971.2'02   74–32137
ISBN 0–395–20280–9

With love for my sister, Nancy, who more than anyone else
shared with me the surprise and wonder of prairie seasons
as a child — who has added to that surprise and wonder a
sense of awe and love for the Creator of those wonders.
Many call it the living whole — ultimate cause — nature.
We two call it: God.

A PRAIRIE BOY'S SUMMER

1. Practicing for Field Day

In June, which westerners really regard as the beginning of summer, school was drawing to a close. William half regretted it, for summer always meant a lot of farm work, a lot more than in winter. At school there were three play recesses. True, it was also exam time; but he was always top of his class and the teacher sometimes even let him do his studying out in the grass by his lonesome.

One thing about June that William didn't look forward to was field day. On the very last school day his school got together with two others in the district to decide which of the three would win The Shield that year for athletic strength and skill. In the last two weeks, training for it got really serious, and the teacher took time off to direct and record her pupils' progress.

There was no way to hide the fact that kids even younger than William could run faster and jump further and higher than he could. So he preferred the novelty races like the sack race, the three-legged race or the wheelbarrow race. He even liked the undignified peanut race in which the contestants had to get down on all fours and push a peanut along the ground with their noses. But William had one consolation. His school rivals during the rest of the year were now on his side. He knew they wanted him to do well in the competitions so The Shield could be won for their school.

2. Softball

In the summer it seemed to William that they played baseball at school every day. They used a softball, which is about twice the size of a hard ball; but though it was softer, it still stung William's more delicate hands, especially when it was new. He didn't care for baseball any more than he did for hockey because he wasn't as quick or strong as other boys his age. Of the various ball games the children played, he preferred less competitive ones like "bat'er-up" or "21 and in." When sides were chosen for baseball even some of the small kids had to play since there were usually only about twenty-five children attending that one-room country schoolhouse. William usually offered to play what he thought was an unimportant position, like second base or mid-field. Standing there he would daydream of making a sensational catch — gaining the respect and admiration of the others. As he stood there he suddenly had to snap back to reality, for someone had hit the ball and it was high in the air heading for near mid-field. The opposing team yelled, "Miss it!" "Miss it!" There were even some cat-calls to rile him! "Butterfingers!" "You can't catch!" He ran under the ball and made a flying leap with arms outstretched. The sun was in his eyes. Do you think he caught it?

3. School Lunch Under the Woodpile

In winter the children had to eat their sometimes-frozen lunch sandwiches at their school desks, but in summer they had a bigger choice of places to eat. One of the boys' favorite spots was under the school woodpile. It offered just the right amount of shade if it was hot, and it cut down the wind that tugged at their lunch wrapping.

William was a rather fussy eater and wasn't always excited about the contents of his lunch box. He always seemed to be getting peanut butter stuck to the roof of his mouth, or corn syrup. Or homemade jam, which had soaked right through the bread by lunch time. Or else hard-boiled eggs that choked him. Or else the butter was too thick. He did like baloney as long as the bread hadn't been soaked by too much French mustard. Real British Columbian apples, brought by his father from town once in a long while, were a treat. Just the smell that rose out of the box on opening it was wonderful.

William was fond of dessert, probably because it wasn't often to be found in his lunch box. When he was smaller and his mother baked a cake, she'd let him scrape out the mixing bowl.

At lunch time, a thermos of milk helped the sandwiches to go down. The thermos was brought in the black, worker's type lunch box that John and he had to share. They envied some of the fancy sandwiches — like brown sugar on butter — of their poorer neighbors. And sometimes they even persuaded them to swap.

4. The Field Day

William could not escape it — the day of the "picnic" or "field day" came. If his school was to compete at one of the other schools, they were driven there in the back of a farm truck. If field day was held at their own school, they walked. The officials were usually the teachers and several of the school trustees. Competition was by age or sex or grade. A starting line was made in the grass with lime, and the finish line was a tightly held string. All competitors' toes were on the line as the official called out, "One for the money. Two for the show. Three to get ready. And four to GO!" Away went everyone. William could see the backs of the fast runners pulling away from him. If he could hear some slower unfortunate clomping along behind, he took comfort.

A lot of parents came and there was a noontime picnic for all in the shade behind the school. After lunch there were jumping and novelty races. Of the winners the first got fifteen cents, the second ten cents and the third five cents. They also earned a certain number of points for their school. Losers like William had to bring money from home to spend in the confection booth — built out of poplar branches — located against an outside wall of the school barn. At the wheelbarrow race William heard someone shout: "Hey, look at that pair out front. The barrow's being carried! He's just pretending to touch the ground. Disqualify them!"

The day ended with two baseball games. The team that won twice usually took the trophy for the year, because a ball game brought a school the most points. William's school won The Shield most often. It didn't seem exactly fair, for William's school also usually had the most pupils.

5. Swallows Dive-Bombing the Cat

The first cat they had on that farm was given a Ukrainian name, "Kitka" — the cat.
William remembered her playing round the stove when she was only a kitten.
She was to produce many litters in all the seven years that she lived — seven is a
ripe old age for a farm cat. So she had a special warm spot in the family's
heart, and she was tolerated in the farm house. All other cats had to live in the barn.

When Kitka saw William's mother preparing to go to the barn at milking time she'd
set out ahead of her knowing there would soon be fresh warm milk for all.
However, barn swallows also lived in the barn and had built their nests there. The
nests were half-cones of mud glued to the side of the ceiling beams, really close to
the ceiling. A cat hadn't the slightest chance of reaching the baby swallows unless
one of the babies by chance fell out on the floor.

But the swallows, William was amused to note, hated even the sight of the enemy.
When Kitka was still a good ways off in the yard the swallows would begin
dive-bombing her. Wheeling into formation high in the air, they'd zoom down to
within a foot of her head, screaming rude swallow words into her ears. Kitka's tail
would twitch angrily but she kept right on her course, pretending not to notice.
She was plotting none-the-less. William could see that, because once in a while she'd
make a leap into the air and try to paw one of the bombers to the ground. Kitka
never succeeded, for the swallows were too fast for her.

While the swallows were dive-bombing, John, Winnie and William were at the barn
riling up the cows at the door so they'd drop their droppings outside instead of in
the barn. But they had to take care not to make the cows so nervous that they'd
withhold their milk during milking.

6. Catching Baby Killdeer

One milking time when William and John were helping their mother in the garden, she sent them to fetch the herd while she finished hoeing the weeds on the last row of cabbages. The boys loved birds so they made sure the herd wouldn't step on a killdeer's nest they knew of near the barn road. A killdeer's nest lies flat, naked and exposed on the ground, but this one was so cleverly camouflaged that William was only able to find it by outsmarting the mother bird. One time when he happened to be passing by she'd flown up and fallen to the ground some yards away, crying and fluttering, pretending her wing was broken. He knew that the more fuss she made the closer he must be to her nest.

This evening, however, when the herd again scared the mother off her nest, William was delighted to see that the eggs had hatched! Darling fluffy little bits of life standing high on legs thinner than toothpicks were scattering in all directions. Not yet able to fly, they tripped on blades of grass and were easily caught. In his hand William could feel the teeny heart going pit-a-pat. He knelt there trying to soothe it by stroking and talking, "Please, please, believe me! I'm not going to hurt you. I just want to hold you for a minute because I love you." How he wished he could tell the frantic mother in bird language that he wouldn't dream of harming her lovable babies.

William was interrupted by his mother's shout from the garden — "Hey, get those cows in!" William let the bird go, knowing that its family would reunite at the nest when they felt it was safe again.

7. Pasturing Cows

Before his father got prosperous enough to put an electric fence around temporary pastures, William often had to pasture cows all day. This wasn't a bad job if the cows were satisfied, for then he could read the pulpy western novels Steve had lent him at school and daydream that he was one of the heroes of the American frontier.

But faraway fields always look greener to a cow, and sometimes, even when William was sure the pasture offered them enough to eat, the herd grew pesky. He'd have sworn they even plotted escape, for they seemed to be only pretending to graze as they moved right up to a grain or corn field. Then, even before William could read another line of the western to find out if his hero had escaped an ambush, the "ornery critters" had crossed the forbidden line and were reveling in "the real thing." If the farm dog stayed with him, his help was appreciated.

Sometimes William tried ambushing the cows to teach them a lesson. He'd hide at the edge of the cornfield, and as soon as he could hear the clicking of ankles and snort-like heavy breathing of a grazing herd, he knew he was close enough to let fly with his slingshot. Sometimes the lead cow, which he'd struck in the forehead with a pebble, would raise her head in the air and shake it about as if dazed. William would fall into a brief panic. "Had he permanently injured her? What would his parents say?" But no, she soon rejoined the rest of the retreating herd and he'd have peace for half an hour or so before "the lesson" had worn off. Then the herd once more pretended to be in grazing formation and headed for the forbidden field.

8. Burning Quack Grass and Harrowing

William got acquainted with other western weeds besides the ones often found in the garden. Every summer when the weather got hot and dry, which was in between the critical seasons of sowing and harvest, it was a good time to summer fallow. This meant working the land that was resting from bearing crops.

Usually the land was plowed first. This buried the grasses and the weeds so that they died and their thick vegetation turned into a kind of fertilizer. Then the land was worked over with harrows, discs, or spring-tooth cultivators to pull out any weeds that survived the plowing. The hot sun and wind dried them out.

The toughest weed to kill was called "quack grass" or "couch grass." Its roots were long and string-like and these would catch onto the soil even though they were torn out and lying on the surface. If there was enough moisture the quack grass would grow both roots and green shoots, and if you left it alone long enough it soon formed a whole colony or patch in the field.

So quack grass roots had to be harrowed or raked together to be burned. It was a tiring, dusty job walking after the harrows all day and William's shoulder ached from lifting harrows clogged with roots. Stacking and burning the piles of grass roots left by the harrows was more fun.

There was the excitement of gambling in it too. Although William had a box of matches in his pocket, he tried to avoid the trouble of starting a fresh fire. Carrying fire on his pitchfork from one pile to another, he had to run to get it across in time — but not so fast that his speed would blow the fire out.

In the far-off distance William could see clumps of bushes quivering and floating as if in a vast lake. This was a heat mirage. And the little whirlwinds that sprang up now and then in the field had an odd Ukrainian name: "a devil's wedding."

9. Haying

Haying was an important early summer job on dairy farms. When his father went into dairying William had to learn many of the steps necessary to make a haystack out of a field of grass. His father planted grass, but his neighbors rented sections of the bog to the east and cut natural grass. William envied the neighbors' boys, for they sometimes stayed out on the bog for two whole weeks cooking out in the open and sleeping under the wagon just like gypsies. He could see their stacker machine throwing hay up onto huge stacks on the horizon. William's father had no stacker, so their stacks were hand built and low.

The first machine that was used in haying was the mower, and it had to be oiled often. Its steady clatter used to put William to sleep. Things like almost cutting a frog in half with the mower blade helped to keep him awake — and in wet years there were many frogs.

William liked the scent of fresh mown hay. The unpleasantness really began when the hay was dry and had to be raked in bundles — first one way, then the other.

The next step, called sweeping, William never did do, for John tried it one day and had an accident. The sweeper was like a giant comb on wheels between two horses. It pushed the hay bundles to the center of the field so that a stack could be built there. The horses were jittery because of horseflies and had to wear wire baskets to protect their tender noses. John's horses bolted from the horseflies, pulling the sweeper with its load of hay so fast that it overturned and rode over him. Only the hay into which he fell saved him.

William had to learn to build the stack properly and at the same time catch more bundles of hay being thrown up by his father and mother. Once, after they had begun building a stack of clover, an approaching thunderstorm during the night forced the family to get up at 2 A.M. to put a peak on the stack. They finished just before the downpour and returned to the house at dawn, looking like drowned rats.

10. Thunderstorm Approaching

William loved the excitement of a thunderstorm during the day. After a hot sultry morning it sometimes came in the afternoon. This day his mother had been watching the dark cloud forming and beginning its swift approach. She yelled to the children, "Go round and close all the doors in the yard! Get the poultry in!" She was raising turkeys as well as geese and chickens that year. Turkeys are not as stupid as chickens and can be herded more easily. Winnie and William went after them.

The dark sky seemed to crack open with a vivid, crooked dagger of lightning. William instinctively drew in his neck, knowing that when a storm was that close it meant the thunder-clap would follow hard on the flash. It came — whomp! The earth almost seemed to tremble from the crash. He liked the after-rumble, which was the echo resounding between earth and heaven as it moved off.

It was only at night that thunderstorms really used to frighten him. On the prairies they sometimes lasted all night. Even though the house had lightning rods on it, he still didn't trust them to keep the lightning from setting fire to the house.

Of course William knew the farm safety rule about not standing under a tree for shelter from a storm. Yet when they were stooking, it was a big temptation to avoid a soaking by heading for the clump of very tall trees that stood across the road. William had actually been hit once when he was closing a gate during the first few drops of rain. Fortunately it wasn't too big a jolt, for it had already traveled a mile down the barbed wire fence. William dropped the gate and ran.

11. Corn Cultivating

In the district where William grew up, corn was raised by dairy farmers for ensilage. The livestock ate the stalk of the corn, not the cobs. There was even a special hybrid corn that produced little or no cobs. It had to be cut while still green, chopped up and put into a silo or ensilage hole before it had all dried out. It could then ferment from its own moisture and weight. But, first, during the summer, while the corn was still only a foot high, it had to be hilled and weeded. William's father bought a new cultivator to do the job and after he himself had learned how to work the machine, he put William on it.

William didn't like farm machines because the monotony of their operation tended to put him to sleep. But he had to be alert on this job, for if his shoe slipped on one of the two foot levers he'd find to his dismay that the set of shovels below were digging up corn instead of weeds.

After William was well practiced on the cultivator he could indulge in some daydreams for relief. One of his dreams was of being surrounded by a group of city high school students listening in admiration to his stories of the adventures of a farm boy. His father had told him that when he passed grade nine he and John would go to a high school in the big city. How mistaken his daydreams were to be! Those city boys weren't in the least interested in nature. So it was to be many, many years before William found a way to get people interested in his stories.

12. Milking Time

Milking was another job William didn't look forward to, especially on hot, fly-filled days. Outside, the blue sky overhead and, perhaps, a refreshing breeze made the inside of the barn seem like a prison. To get at the teats on the far side of the cow's udder he was forced to lean tight against the cow's belly, which heaved and radiated heat like a big furnace. And to add to the discomfort of the sweat, flies used his head and hands as a landing field.

Also William had to be ready to grab the pail of milk away in case the cow kicked at a fly and put her foot in the pail. She used her tail as a fly swatter, too; and its coarse, dirty hairs often slapped William right across the back of the neck. True, he did spray the cow with flytox, but its effect soon wore off. It was best when his little sister Nancy held the tail.

As relief from the milking ordeal William would sometimes amuse himself by squirting a barn cat that was waiting nearby, meowing for its evening ration of milk. First that cat would jump away as if upset. But really it liked the shower, for it immediately sat down further off and set about licking away the milk.

William's mother was the best milker. But if his parents were away for some reason it meant John and he had ten cows each to milk. Their wrists ached that night so they got little sleep. Everybody heaved a sigh of relief when the family became prosperous enough to buy a set of milking machines.

13. The Swimming Hole

William, like many another prairie boy, never saw a large body of water till his mid-teens. He did have a place to swim, though, for one summer the older boys of the district had widened out one place in the bog ditch to the east of his father's farm. They built a sod dam and even a rough diving platform. It was the neighborhood swimming hole from then on.

Since no adult had helped out by putting sand on the bottom, the boys had to settle for clay and mud. They could feel it squishing up between their toes, but they couldn't see it. As soon as they jumped into the water they raised clouds of clay sediment that made the water as opaque as pea soup. William didn't dare open his eyes under such water.

None of the boys brought towels, so when the sun dried their bodies off they found they had a fine, white coating of clay, which could be brushed off. By late afternoon, when they all headed home for milking, they saw that the clay cloud they'd raised had flowed as far as the first bridge.

William disliked two colonies of water creatures that lived at either end of the swimming hole. Black catfish, with their peculiar black whiskers, hung around out of curiosity at the clear upper end. The dam at the lower end was like an apartment for dozens of crayfish.

William loathed the thought of stepping on a crayfish but couldn't resist raising the sod once in a while to stare at them. Sometimes as a joke one of these "crabs" or a frog would be put in some swimmer's shoe.

Another trick was to hide a swimmer's clothes. This was rather mean because they all swam stark naked so the victim would be left with nothing to wear. To dry off, the boys ran around in the big field opposite the hole and let the sun and wind do the job. No one lived way out on the bog, but they kept one quarter of an eye open, for once in a rare while a gang of local girls did visit the bog on their bikes.

14. Making a Smudge

Apart from milking, dairying was much easier in summer than winter. During the day, except for having to pump a tankful of water for the cows, the boys could let them look after themselves. On some summer days, especially in the wetter years, there was one more favor the cattle appreciated from William. This was when his parents sent him out at sunset to build a smudge fire to protect the animals from mosquitoes. There were clouds of these pests; everyone said they came off the bog.

William found there were really no gentlemen in the animal world. Even if the cows got to the smudge first, the horses always came along and took away the smokiest places. The cows knew horses were bullies, so they moved out of the way before they were bitten or pushed aside.

A smudge was not the same as a bonfire though it was sometimes called that. William's father showed him how to make a smudge by mixing layers of dry straw with layers of wet straw or manure so that the pile would glow and smoke instead of blaze. Otherwise the fire would burn out long before daylight and the cattle were left unprotected. Of course, if there was no breeze the smoke didn't help much, for it went straight up. But that didn't happen very often.

15. Plowing

Plowing was a long, lonely job. On the old tractor William didn't fall asleep so easily because its steel wheels made the ride very rough. But the new tractor had rubber tires, and there was only the noise of its two cylinders to keep him awake. "Bach, Bach — Bach, Bach," its exhaust repeated over and over all day long and even after supper till it was completely dark. As long as William could still make out the furrow, he could plow.

William's father had adjusted the plow levers for the right depth, and because the tractor was new, it hardly ever broke down. The only excuse for stopping was when Nancy brought out some water or lunch. Or if the fuel was low. William didn't dare turn the motor off because he hadn't learned the knack of turning the flywheel to start it up again. One time, after turning the flywheel for two hours and getting blisters all over his hands, he had to go out on the bog to get his friend Billie to help him.

Also William was still not strong enough to tip a fuel barrel to fill the fuel can. Instead he had to siphon the distillate. Distillate was a cheaper, less refined fuel than gasoline and was used only in tractors. At first he used to siphon by sucking on the end of the hose. But he didn't like the taste of distillate if he happened to get a mouthful of it. Another way to get the siphon going, if he were lucky, was to hold his hand tightly over the outside end of the hose. Then he'd quickly pull that end up and into the fuel can and remove his hand. Sometimes the fuel flowed into his can.

Making turns on the tractor was easy enough after the first year of bungling. William also got the knack of pulling the trip rope, to raise the plow when he reached the end of the furrow, or to drop it after making the "E" turn. A flock of gulls followed William as he plowed, ready to gobble up the worms and other bugs the plow might turn up.

16. Cutting Grain

William was only twelve when his father drafted him and John into harvest work. He might have had another year or two to grow stronger, more capable if the war had not come and taken away all his father's hired hands. William knew it was war because bombers began to appear in the sky from the direction of the city airfield. They would drop their bomb loads far out on the bog to the east and then circle back over the farm toward the city.

At first William was put on the old black tractor pulling two binders, with his father on the front one, and John on the second. They were old binders and broke down a lot, so William always had to be ready to make a quick stop when his father yelled "Whoa!" To make up time lost fixing the equipment they had to cut grain on into the night, even after the moon rose. William and John were so dead-tired at bed time that they dropped off to sleep without even washing off the field dust.

The second year was easier. By then the old tractor had broken down completely and his father had bought a new, bright green one. Now when things were going well they could even look around a bit and enjoy nature.

One amusement was to see all the creatures that would run out of the patch of uncut grain in the middle of the field. As the patch got smaller and smaller more and more creatures appeared — partridges, gophers, rabbits, skunks. The farm dog would be on hand then, waiting for the game, though he rarely caught anything. Rabbits ran too fast, and he had learned by painful experience not to get too close to a skunk.

Nancy was just strong enough by then to carry water out to the workers in the field. It was hot, dry work.

17. Stooking

Some years there were wet spells even during harvest time. It would not actually rain — just turn foggy and drizzly — but too much moisture is not good for the grain. Wet grain or grain that had sprouted in the stocks was good only for feed. Gray weather made William sad.

If the grain was too wet to cut the family could still stook. William's mother, who was a good stooker, taught William how to do it properly. You picked up two sheaves, holding them by the binder twine or under your arms, and brought them firmly to the ground with their tops together, leaning against each other. Then another pair of sheaves were brought down in the same way, on either side of the first two, to complete the stook. A stook had a hole through the middle so the wind could dry it from inside as well as out, and it was shaped like a teepee so the rain would run off.

When stooking, everyone wore long sleeves and, if possible, trousers and even gloves to protect themselves from stubble and straw scratches. William hated barley because the sheaves were small and sometimes fell apart, their beards scratching his face. The worst thing was getting a barley beard in the mouth or throat. It irritated like anything, and it took some fishing with one's fingers to get it out.

In wet years there were more mice. They had to be killed because of all the grain they ate. This put some excitement into the work. William and Mother heard John yell out, "A mouse!" and saw him (and sometimes the dog) chasing after it. Sometimes the mouse might succeed in hiding in the next row of sheaves, but sooner or later they got it when that row was being stooked.

18. Mending Pig's Fence

Because pigs are such notorious wanderers, they had to be penned inside a page-wire fence. They are also notorious rooters, so every few days they'd dig under the fence and escape. It seemed that a large part of William's life on the farm was spent capturing escapees. Horses, bulls, chickens, calves, pigs, all had their "prison breaks." It was hard herding pigs back after a breakout. To begin with, one couldn't be sure where they'd gone. As a last resort there was one advantage William's family always had; most escapees eventually got hungry and came back to be fed.

But the family found an even cleverer way to get the pig herd back. If one of the pigs was left in the pen, father would twist its leg or ear and it would squeal "blue murder" — loud and long. A pig's hearing is very sharp. Soon William would see the whole herd come charging back from the other end of the farm to defend the brother in distress. As soon as they'd rushed in through the open gate or through the hole they'd dug, the innocent one would be released from his tortures.

Then William and John had the job of repairing the fence. While the boys worked, the pigs stood at a distance in the weeds, sniffing and snorting and watching with their mischievous little eyes. "Look at the rascals," said William. "You'd swear it's more than curiosity. I bet they're studying how to undo this repair job!"

19. Gopher Hunting

School always opened on the first of September. All through the summer holidays
the schoolhouse seemed to be sleeping, resting from the beating that a boisterous
bunch of country kids had given it in the past and would again give it in the fall.
Free from trampling young feet, weeds managed to grow high in front of the school
buildings; and out in the tall grass, gophers had dug their burrows.

As soon as a gopher was spotted by the returning kids, a hunting posse was formed.
Maybe city children will think William was a little monster for joining in
enthusiastically. But gophers are pests to farmers, and when there were too many
of them the municipality paid kids a one-cent-a-tail bounty for them. Some of
the posse had stones and clubs. Others carried several pails of water, and often a
dog from the nearby farm joined the chase.

A gopher usually escaped the first pail of water poured down her hole by emerging
from a second, back-door hole. "There she goes," yelled William as she
scampered to another hole. They had to act fast then, for they knew that the
gopher realized she was in danger of water death and had to quickly build a dam
below ground. If she succeeded, the boys always knew it, for only a little water
went in before the hole was full. On the other hand, if bubbles began coming up they
knew they had her. She'd surface, very drowned looking and miserable, and try to
escape by running between the legs of the attackers to still another hole. William
even felt a twinge of pity for her, when she was finished off. But a pest is a pest.

20. Bows and Arrows

Threshing time was a sure sign autumn was taking over after summer. Already there was a certain chill in the air at night. From the school yard William could see bright new straw stacks rising here and there on the farm horizon. His father's were the most numerous, for he still prided himself on being a grain farmer.

A threshing scene is an exciting one, even at a distance. William felt a little guilty enjoying his recess when it was the busiest season on the farm for his parents. But he knew they excused him, for his father thought education even more important than farm work.

William was really happy that the other boys went along with a new sport he introduced — Archery. The kids called it simply "Bows and Arrows." William had a natural knack for carving and found his bows and arrows were the best for distance and accuracy.

At last William could stand straight and tall, for in this one sport he excelled. He read in a book that using the feet to shoot with sent an arrow even further than by hand. So they all sat down to try it, and sure enough it worked.

It seemed to the boys that they were conquering the awesomeness of the prairie expanses at last. The arrow went clear out of the school yard into the pasture on the other side of the highway. In another two years William, too, would be leaving that grassy school yard for the concrete and cinders of a city playground. From there he'd be able to send his "arrows" both to the East and the Far West of this great country that he was born in.